AMAZING
SCIENCE

Sunshine
A Book About Sunlight

by Josepha Sherman   illustrated by Jeff Yesh

Thanks to our advisers for their expertise, research, knowledge, and advice:

Mark W. Seeley, Ph.D., Professor of Meteorology and Climatology
Department of Soil, Water, and Climate
University of Minnesota, St. Paul

Mike Graf, M.A., Instructor of Child Development
Chico (California) State University

Susan Kesselring, M.A., Literacy Educator
Rosemount-Apple Valley-Eagan (Minnesota) School District

PICTURE WINDOW BOOKS
Minneapolis, Minnesota

Managing Editor: Bob Temple
Creative Director: Terri Foley
Editors: Sara E. Hoffmann, Michael Dahl
Editorial Adviser: Andrea Cascardi
Copy Editor: Laurie Kahn
Designer: Nathan Gassman
Page production: Picture Window Books
The illustrations in this book were rendered digitally.

Picture Window Books
5115 Excelsior Boulevard
Suite 232
Minneapolis, MN 55416
1-877-845-8392
www.picturewindowbooks.com

Printed in the United States of America.

Library of Congress Cataloging-in-Publication Data
Sherman, Josepha.
Sunshine : a book about sunlight / by Josepha Sherman ;
illustrated by Jeff Yesh. v. cm. — (Amazing science)
Includes bibliographical references and index.
Contents: We need sunlight—Sun and Earth—
Daytime—Sun and weather—Rainbows—Sunset—
Night and moonlight—Another day.
ISBN 1-4048-0096-4
1. Sunshine—Juvenile literature. [1. Sunshine.]
I. Yesh, Jeff, 1971—ill. II. Title.
QC911.2 .S48 2003
551.5'271—dc21
                                            2003004711

Table of Contents

Summer sunlight shines down on the beach.

Bright waves sparkle like dancing jewels.

The hot sand warms your bare feet.

Ice cream melts, and candy turns sticky.

Your skin feels warm and dry.

4

5

Sun and Earth

The sun is a giant ball of gas that warms and lights the earth. Earth is smaller than the sun. The earth spins like a top in space.

The sun seems to rise into the air in the morning, cross the sky at midday, and sink back down at night. Even though the sun looks as if it is moving, it always stays in the same place. Instead, it is the earth that moves. When one side of the earth faces the sun, the other side faces away from it.

Daytime

When a place on earth faces the sun,
people living in that area say it is daytime.
As the sun first appears in that part of the world,
it is called morning.

During the day, sunlight shines on
tiny water droplets, bits of dust, and
the gases that make up the air around us.
The sunlight is scattered by these tiny particles
and gases, and it spreads across the sky.
The scattered light makes the sky look blue.

9

We Need Sunlight

Without the sun, our world would be wrapped
in darkness. Trees, grass, and other plants
would not grow. Animals and people
would have nothing to eat.

Without the heat from sunlight,
oceans and lakes would turn to ice.
The air would be very still
and too cold to breathe.

Sun and Weather

The sun creates our weather. Oceans, lakes, and rivers take in energy from sunlight. This energy heats the water. When the water gets warm, some of it turns into vapor. The vapor rises and mixes with the air. As water vapor cools, it turns into tiny droplets that form clouds. These clouds can bring rain or snow.

The land also absorbs sunlight's energy. As the land warms up, it heats the air above it. Warm air rises and expands. As the air moves, a breeze is formed. These winds rush across lakes and fields, cities and mountains.

Rainbows

Spray a garden hose into the air.
Watch the sunlight hit the streaming water.
The water droplets catch the light and
scatter it, breaking it into different colors.
A rainbow glistens.

During a rainstorm, sunlight can form a rainbow in the sky. If enough water droplets fall, a double rainbow may appear.

Sunset

When a place on earth begins to turn away from the sun, people living there say night is coming. As the sun appears to set, it is called dusk.

The sun seems low in the sky. The sunlight has more air and particles to shine through. Now the light turns the sky a fiery red, deep orange, or soft pink. Soon, the sky turns velvety blue, then deep, dark blue, then black.

Night and Moonlight

Night comes and stars flicker like faraway candles.

The stars cannot be seen during the daytime.

The sun shines more brightly than the stars and hides them.

At night, the moon gleams with a pale, cool glow. Moonlight really comes from the sun. Part of the moon's surface faces the sun. This part of the moon catches the sun's light. Some of the light bounces off the moon and shines down to earth.

Another Day

The spinning earth makes the moon and stars seem to change positions slowly in the sky.

Soon the night sky begins to brighten.
Stars turn pale and disappear.
The tops of tall mountains
and buildings begin to glow.

When the sun appears, another day begins.

You Can Make a Rainbow

What you need:

- water
- a clear drinking glass
- a beam of sunlight
- a piece of white paper

What you do:

1. Make sure you have an adult help you.

2. Pour water into the glass until it is half full.

3. Find a very sunny spot in your home or classroom.

4. Place the white piece of paper on a table in the sunlight.

5. Place the glass on the paper.

6. What do you see on the white piece of paper?

Fast Facts

- The sun is a star, just like the ones you see in the night sky. It seems bigger than other stars do, but that is just because it is closer to the earth.

- The sun is so big that it sometimes looks like it is not very far away. The sun is actually 93 million miles (149,637,000 kilometers) from earth.

- One of nature's most interesting events has to do with the sun. This event is called a solar eclipse. A solar eclipse happens when the moon blocks the sun's light. This makes the earth get very dark, even in the middle of the day.

- You should never look directly at the sun. The sun can hurt your eyes, even when it does not seem very bright. It is a good idea to wear sunglasses when you are playing outside, but not even sunglasses can protect your eyes from direct sunlight.

Glossary

breeze—a gentle wind

dusk—the time in the evening when it starts to get dark

expand—to get bigger

gas—something that is not solid or liquid and does not have a definite shape

particle—a very small piece of something, like a grain of dirt

scatter—to separate something into smaller pieces and send it in many different directions

vapor—particles of mist, smoke, or steam

To Learn More

At the Library

Branley, Franklyn M. *The Sun: Our Nearest Star*. New York: HarperCollins, 2002.
Owen, Andy. *Sunshine*. Des Plaines, Ill.: Heinemann Library, 1999.
Rustad, Martha E.H. *The Sun*. Mankato, Minn.: Pebble Books, 2002.

On the Web

For Kids Only: Earth Science Enterprise
http://kids.earth.nasa.gov
For information on NASA and how its scientists study air, water, and land

The National Severe Storms Laboratory's Weather Room
http://www.nssl.noaa.gov/edu
For fun, basic information on weather for kids, parents, and teachers

Fact Hound
Fact Hound offers a safe, fun way to find Web sites related to this book.
All of the sites on Fact Hound have been researched by our staff.
http://www.facthound.com

1. Visit the Fact Hound home page.

2. Enter a search word related to this book,
   or type in this special code: 1404800964.

3. Click on the FETCH IT button.

Your trusty Fact Hound will fetch the best sites for you!

Index